To – Jan –
My Dear Friend – Wish You Were
Here – Merry Christmas 1991,
and a Happy New Year!
Love,
Mary Ann

SEASONAL WREATHS

from Caprilands

Holiday Celebrations with Herbal Wreath Lore and Design

Adelma Grenier Simmons

Photographs by
George Gregory Wieser

MALLARD PRESS

Copyright © 1991 by Adelma Grenier Simmons
Photographs copyright © 1991 by George Gregory Wieser

All rights reserved. No part of this publication may be reproduced or transmitted
in any form or by any means, electronic or mechanical, including photocopy,
recording or any information storage and retrieval system,
without the written permission of the publisher.

Mallard Press and its accompanying design and logo are trademarks of
BDD Promotional Book Company, Inc.
First published in the United States of America in 1991 by Mallard Press,
an imprint of BDD Promotional Book Company, Inc.
666 Fifth Avenue
New York, NY 10103
ISBN 0-7924-5619-X

Editorial Development by Beverly Pennacchini
Design, Typography and Production by Tony Meisel
Photographic Styling by Laurie Pepin
Origination and Printing by
Impresora Donneco International, S.A. de C.V.

Produced by Wieser & Wieser, Inc.
118 East 25th Street, New York, NY 10010

Printed in MEXICO

CONTENTS

Introduction

WREATHS THROUGH THE AGES

Wreath making is one of the ways we can celebrate the stirring of the seasons, and give greater meaning to holidays, and special occasions. Wreaths, and the herbs and flowers of which they are composed, can enrich our appreciation of life.

Wreaths hold significance not only because they are a festive and decorative way to mark a holiday, but also because of their connection to history and to a time when people were far more influenced by the seasons of the growing year and the meaning and uses of herbs.

To ancient Greeks, wreaths were crowns of glory to signify victory, wisdom or rescue from defeat. In the Middle Ages, wreaths were a way to celebrate a saint's day, and individual herbs came to signify a legend from the saint's life. In agricultural communities, wreath making was a way to express hope for a prosperous year, or thanks for a bountiful harvest.

Although for most of the 20th century, the word "wreath" conjures up one vision of an evergreen ring hung upon a door at Christmas time, we at Caprilands have returned to the origins of this craft. As we prepare and shape herbs and flowers into wreaths, their histories and legends enrich the hours and inspire our hands.

A bright and colorful wedding wreath foretells a glorious day.

6

SPRING

May Day

May Day, which during the Middle Ages and the Renaissance fell on May 12th, was a celebration of the arrival of Spring. It was at last warm enough to spend the night in the woods, and the young men and women of the village would return in the morning laden with flowers, boughs, and branches for making garlands and crowns and decking the Maypole.

Villagers built the Maypole from a tall, straight pine or hawthorne, which symbolized their hope for a plentiful harvest. During the celebration, a King and Queen of the May were chosen, and crowned with wreaths of hawthorne, lily of the valley, and daisies. These white blossoms signified new life, and purity.

Daisy Wreath

A fresh wreath of daisies is an appropriate May Day decoration. Few blossoms are more reflective of youth and innocence. Daisy wreaths are made from green, not dried flowers, and inserted into a wet sphagnum moss base. They may be dried in silica gel, however the results are hardly worth the expense and trouble. A fern makes an attractive accent. Daisy wreaths are living wreaths, and must be placed on trays to hold moisture and to make watering possible.

Daisy

Chrysanthemum leucanthemum

The oxeye daisy, the familiar, wild white daisy of the eastern United States, is a European native which has been long naturalized in our

7

fields and pastures. The true English daisy can be grown from seed but must have winter protection. Daisies signify purity in thought and loyal love.

Kitchen Wreath

Kitchen wreaths can be made from any culinary herb that can be removed and used to season foods. Thyme is a good base because it is easy to grow, abundant, and its sweetness lasts long after it has dried. Rosemary, sage, savory, dill and parsley are also good ingredients for a kitchen wreath. Wreaths can be decorated with the edible blossoms of pot marigold. Kitchen wreaths can be arranged upon an edible base of thyme, or bound dill stalks.

Sage
Salvia officinalis

Sage is a hardy perennial. Its firm oval leaves have a pebbly, puckered surface. The stems and leaves have a pungent but pleasant fragrance and are covered with silver gray hairs. In August, purple flowers appear in whorls along the top of the stem. Sage may be grown from seed, division or cuttings and thrives in moderately rich soil and full sun Sage signifies youth, immortality, and domestic virtue.

Miniature wreaths

A good way to use up left over odds and ends is to make some small, six-inch wreaths. For these miniature wreaths, we begin with a base of sweet Annie about two inches thick. Using a glue gun to hold materials in place, we then dot the base with tiny pieces of tansy, amaranthus, miniature strawflowers, and bits of yarrow. These wreaths make delightful fragrant little gifts, or you can place them around candlesticks in table decorations.

Culinary herbs—sage, rosemary or thyme—can be removed from a kitchen wreath and used to season soups or stews.

10

Tansy
Tanacetum Vulgare

Tansy is a hardy perennial with fernlike leaves and yellow button cluster flowers which are everlastings and excellent in fall or winter wreaths. Tansy prefers sun to partial shade in almost any soil and has a tendency to overrun gardens so is best when planted against a fence in a confined area. It was once believed that tansy, used as a tea, cured the measles and came to be a symbol of immortality due to its use by ancient Greeks and Romans at burials.

Heart Shaped Wreath

This is a Victorian wreath which is arranged upon a fine base of the whitest and best silver king artemisia with tips that look like a border of silver lace. To make this wreath, we use a large quantity of strawflowers, which require special wiring, and can be purchased with wires already inserted. If you grow them in your garden, you will have to do this task ahead of time. This wreath also features small yarrows, blue salvia, dried rosebuds, pinks, and lavender flowers. To make the heart shape, bend the base wire into the desired shape, and cover with artemisia.

Rosemary is a perennial evergreen shrub with needle-like, fragrant leaves associated with Christmas. The gingery scent is released when the sun hits the leaves, or when someone brushes the plant. Rosemary should be started from cuttings and can be wintered indoors in a cool window. Harvest sprigs year round. Rosemary signifies constancy, fidelity, loyalty, and remembrance.

11

SUMMER

Midsummer Day

Midsummer Day, June 24th, is the celebration of the summer solstice, when the sun is highest in the sky and nature is at its best. In Medieval times it was celebrated as the feast of John the Baptist. It has long been considered a magical day when fairies and demons might make an unwitting soul invisible, just for sport.

Midsummer is the time of celebration when marriageable girls donned their best and everyone wore festive crowns of special significance. Flowers used in Midsummer celebrations had to be picked before the dew had dried and the sun driven away the magic. Chaplets composed of white lilies and vervain adorned the maiden's heads. Bonfires were built, and the village gathered for traditional dances and songs. Garlands made from mugwort and fennel dressed rafters and doorways to protect against misfortune.

Bridal Crown

Historically, brides wore wreaths as wedding crowns, which became, when dried, a valued heirloom. These crowns might be simple-a slender chaplet braided from wild leaves and flowers, or elaborate-a circlet of silver Russian olive leaves, which symbolized virginity. Today, bridal wreaths can include silk flowers, ribbons, dried flowers and appropriate herbs which, as in the past, were included not only because they symbolized love and innocence, but because they dried well and retained their color.

Far left. This lush rosemary wreath emits a powerful scent of intense herbal nose.

Top left. For Valentine's Day, arrange a Victorian wreath on a heart-shaped base and finish with a red bow.

Bottom left. A colorful dried-flower wreath brings joy throughout the year.

14

Rose
Rosa spp.

The rose, wild or cultivated, is a thorny stemmed, flowering shrub with showy blossoms. Roses can be propagated from seeds, cuttings, or buddings, but it's easiest to buy nursery stock. Roses grow well in well-drained, enriched soil. Roses have always held special meaning for brides as they signify beauty, youth, love, charm and innocence (white) or love and desire (red).

Victorian Wreath

In formal Victorian parlors, wreaths in memory of departed family members adorned table tops and mantles. Despite these solemn origins, Victorian wreaths can be bright, fragrant and dainty. The color scheme of a Victorian wreath can vary, but the most appropriate includes soft pinks, pale yellows, white, light blue, lime green, and all shades of mauve - the prevalent color of this time period known as the "mauve decade." You can tie bits of lavender and sweet violets and lilacs in the knot for fragrance.

Lavender
Lavandula angustifolia

This sweetly fragrant perennial herb is characterized by needle-like gray-green leaves and spikes of lavender flowers. Lavender seed does not always germinate and grows slowly. Take slips of lavender with the heel attached and root in moist sand. Harvest in late June, July and sometimes August. Cut the blossom stem down to where it joins the main body of the plant. Lavender symbolizes undying love, purity, sweetness and cleanliness.

Twining Hops Wreath

Often just a single herb makes a beautiful seasonal wreath. For instance, the pale green female flowers of the twining hops plant makes a distinct wreath that looks pleasant hung in a window or placed around a punch bowl. This fruit dries very well, but shatters easily, so cut it as soon as it is well developed and handle with care.

Twining Hops
Hummulus lupulus

This grain, used in the production of beer, produces a fruit that resembles a Japanese lantern and makes beautiful and exotic accents to mixed wreaths, or looks very attractive on its own. This plant grows frequently in the wild, but can be cultivated as well. The leaves can be lightly boiled and served as a vegetable. Historically small pillows were filled with hop leaves to aid sleep, and are still served as a tea to aid sleeplessness.

Desdemona's Lament

Coiled willow leaves inserted in a base of sweet Annie accent this autumn wreath, combined with the brilliant fall shades of tansy, goldenrod, orange calendulas, and scarlet nigella pods. The possibilities for autumn wreaths seem endless.

Willow
Salix spp.

Willows vary in size. The weeping willow is well known for its graceful, pendulant branches. Willows seek water and grow best in moist environments. Cut the pliable branches whenever you need them. Pussy willow branches may be harvested in spring when the catkins appear. A willow signifies sorrow.

16

Top right. A living wreath of fresh mugwort daisies makes an excellent May Day decoration.

Bottom right. This summer floral wreath blushes with color.

Far right. Bridal crowns are composed of herbs and flowers symbolic of love and innocence.

18

Artemisia
Artemisia spp.

Varieties of artemisia include mugwort, silver king, sweet Annie and wormwood. The plants provide profuse quantities of feathery plums. Most have silvery foliage, but some are brownish gray or yellow green.Artemisia's are more easily grown from cuttings and root divisions than from seed. They self-sow, so be sure to pull out seedlings growing where you do not want them. Harvest in the middle of September, but leave some for later. Artemisia signifies dignity and protection from disease and misfortune.

AUTUMN

Lammas Day

Lammas Day, August 1, originated with the worship of Ceres, goddess of planting and harvesting. On this day, the first grains of the harvest were baked into bread as an offering to the goddess. In medieval times, Lammas Day was a time to dedicate the first fruits of the harvest to the church in thanksgiving for the abundance of the growing season.

Lammas Day Wreath

Italian bearded wheat makes a lovely Lammas Day celebration wreath when attached to a base of artemisia. For accent, select a dried flower with a glowing autumn shade, such as the pot marigold.

Pot Marigold
Calendula officinalis

Pot marigolds are of varying shades of yellow and orange and open at dawn and close in the morning. This type of marigold is not related to the marigolds planted in flower gardens. Grow pot marigolds from seed, but be certain your seed is fresh. Marigolds bloom more quickly in rich soil and will survive light frost. Pick at noon when they are fully open. This flower signifies joy and the raising of gloomy spirits.

Oak leaves, to the ancient Greeks and Romans, were a symbol of valour and strength. To early agrarians, oak leaves posessed the power to discourage withcraft. During harvest season, wreaths of untreated oak are a pleasant addition to any door or rafter. This wreath is made on a base of artemisia annua and decorated with acorns.

Far left. Lammas Day wreaths are composed of bearded wheat that traditionally symbolized the first grains of the harvest.

Left. Witch's wreaths include plants such as smoky clematis that were believed to discourage witchcraft.

Oak
Quercus spp.

A large, common American shade tree with lobed leaves. Oaks can be propagated from seeds sown in autumn in rich, moist soil. Gather leaves in autumn for their color. Oak symbolizes protection from witchcraft and other evil spirits.

Witch's Wreath

The witch's wreath represents the many plants that both attract and repel witchcraft. Some essential plants to include are rue, wild geranium, willow, hawthorne, elder, smoky clematis, which imparts the smoky, ghostly look to the center of this wreath, and bitter sweet berries. All of these plants, historically, were thought to aid the farmer in warding off trickster spirits, and were hung on door frames and from rafters during the harvest season.

Bittersweet
Celestrus scadens

This plant grows most commonly in the wild. Bittersweet should be cut as soon as the leaves drop and the fruit turns yellow. Usually they are ready in late August or early September. Collect branches when the berries have their yellow husks still on and before they open; do not wait for frost. Bring the branches indoors and hang them overnight. The yellow pods will open and expose the beautiful orange-red fruit. Harvested this way, the outer yellow shell will not drop off. Bittersweet belongs to the poisonous nightshade family, so do not use its fruit or leaves for anything but decorations.

Autumn Floral Wreath

The muted shades of autumn are combined in the dried floral wreath. The hushed golden tones of yarrow, goldenrod and salvia, combine with nigella pods,thistles, or dock seeds to create a whispery, harvest festival look. The base is made from silver king artemisia.

Highlight herb: Yarrow

This hardy perennial has gray-green leaves and flowers which range from pale lavender to golden yellow. These plants prefer full sun and well drained soil. Historically, yarrow was used by Achilles to treat his wounded soldiers and is still used in treating fevers, colds and kidney disorders.

Far left. A wreath of hops—the same that go to bitter beer and ale—makes an unusual summer decoration.

Top left. Yarrow, goldenrod and thistle make an inviting, year-round wreath.

Bottom left. Lemon verbena makes a wreath to fill the room with spicy lemon scent.

WINTER

St. Martin's Day

St. Martin's Day, November 11th, is the first saint's day of the Christmas holiday season, and traditionally begins Advent observances. Historically, it was also the time of year that farmers slaughtered their livestock and salted the meat to eat during the winter. It was the time for feasting and fond farewells when hired farm workers left for their homes or winter work.

St. Martin's Wreath

Our St. Martin's wreath begins with a circle of braided straw, wrapped with embroidered Swedish woven binding. We add sprigs of boxwood to give the holiday look and wire small lady apples into the straw base for color and to signify the harvest. A bow of boxwood finishes the design.

Boxwood

Buxus sempervirens

An evergreen shrub or tree with many small, dark green, lustrous leaves. Boxwood grows well in ordinary, well-drained soil and thrives in shade or sun. It is best propagated from hardwood cuttings. Set new plants in the ground in late summer or early spring. Boxwood signifies immortality and was traditionally dedicated to the god Pluto, who symbolized the continuation of life in the infernal regions.

St. Nicholas' Wreath

Our St. Nicholas' wreath may be made with either evergreens or artemisia as a base. To signify the Dutch saint's famous bags of gold handed out to dowerless daughters, we like to add golden flowers such as yarrow, tansy or broom. St. Nicholas' Day is also the time when cookies are baked and we often wire interesting cookie cutters to our wreath to add brightness. We finish with small bunches of spices such as cinnamon sticks and nutmeg.

Cinnamon
Cinnamonum zeylanicum

Cinnamon, a member of the laurel family, is a spicy bark which was once a chief ingredient in the preparation of holy oils. The cinnamon tree, native to Ceylon, India, Malaya, China and the East Indies, grows to 30 feet and is propagated from seeds. Cinnamon is made from the inner bark cut into cylinders from young trees.

Advent Wreath

Bind a generous amount of sphagnum moss to a ring or frame so that once wet, it will hold enough moisture for the living herbs. Force branches of juniper, with berries if possible, into the frame to make a good circle. To the base we add symbolic herbs appropriate to the season: rosemary, pennyroyal, mint, thyme and lavender. Next we add the candles. Around the candles we group dried statice, white globe amaranths and silver cuttings of santolinas. Placed on a metal tray and watered, this Advent wreath will last through December and well into January

Top right. A spice wreath brings forth memories of fresh-baked delicacies.

Bottom right. Holiday spices such as nutmeg and cinnamon add a holiday flair to this St. Nicholas wreath.

Far right. Lady apples embellish a St. Martin's wreath, finished with embroidered binding.

Juniper
Juniperus sabina

A valued evergreen whose spreading branches are covered with silvery blue berries. Juniper grows wild in pastures and woodlands, and prefers a light, loamy soil and full sun. Both male and female shrubs must be grown for the female to produce berries. Juniper drives away witches and provides protection.

Herb and Spice Wreath

After making a base from artemisia, attach a ring of bay, wired together in flat bunches of three or four so that they can be removed to season soups or sauces. In the center of each bunch of bays, fasten three whole nutmegs, cinnamon sticks, and cardamom. Finally, add the typical herbs and spices of the holiday season in small cellophane bags for easy removal. Anise, caraway, coriander and rue can be tied to the wreath under a velvet bow.

Bay
Laurus nobilis

A tender perennial with beautiful dark green leaves which are mildly fragrant and very flavorful. Propagate bay from cuttings which take about six months to root. Thrives in partial shade and grows well in tubs as a city tree,as its thick leaves resist pollution. Bay is a mark of achievement, distinction and superiority. It reputedly protects against the ravages of thunder and lightening.

MAKING WREATHS

Harvest and Preservation

The first step in wreath construction is to obtain the materials. You should prepare and assemble more material than you think you will need, so that you will not have to halt progress on a wreath project to replenish supplies. One sure way to be assured of having plenty of herbs is to grow your own, but you can also gather wild plants from the countryside. In the fall, you can find many plants and seed pods that have dried in the fields and are ready for use. You can also purchase wreath materials in craft stores, florist shops and country markets.

The best time to pick material for wreath making is late morning. By that time, the sun has dried the dew but hasn't leached out the colors or the essential oils that keep perfumes intact and leaves and petals looking fresh.

Flower color is brightest when blossoms first open. Many flowers will continue opening after they have been cut, so make allowances for this. Some flowers, such as strawflowers, should be checked everyday. The general rule for harvesting flowers is to cut blooms when they are fully formed but the centers are still tightly closed. With experience, you will learn the best harvest times for each plant you use.

Heavy stemmed plants, such as willow, bittersweet, honeysuckle and grapevines, should be stripped of leaves as soon as they are picked and then formed immediately into wreath bases while they are still pliable.

Dried herbs and flowers form the basis for hundreds of wreath variants.

Although you will use certain herbs and flowers right away to make living wreaths, most of the materials you will use in wreaths and garlands will have to be dried or preserved in some way. The importance of a dry, dark, well-ventilated room for drying both foliage and flowers cannot be too strongly emphasized. Sun leaches the color out of many fine materials, and dampness causes mold and mildew. Attics, lofts, balconies, garages, or other high places with good air circulation make ideal drying areas.

Many herbs can be dried by hanging in bunches. If you won't be using the leaves, strip them from the stems as they are a source of moisture, which encourages mold. Tie the stems together in loose bunches, so that air circulates among them. As plants dry, the stems shrivel and may have to be re-tied. If you are not planning to use the material immediately, protect it from dust as well as light.

Large stems that will be used for wreath bases are often best dried in baskets. The stems of artemisia dry straight and very stiff when they are hung, but placed loosely in baskets when stems are fresh and pliable, they will droop over the edge as they dry and bend into gently curling shapes. They are then much easier to fashion into wreaths.

Rosebuds and other flowers that will be wired should be dried well in a single layer on trays or screens. Place these screens away from light in an airy spot. Decorative seedpods harvested from the garden or the fields can also be dried in this manner if they are not already thoroughly dry when you gather them. To dry flowers with flat blossoms, such as Queen Anne's lace, puncture holes in the top of a box; then thread the stems through the holes so the flower heads rest on the lid.

Many flowers dry best when placed in a drying medium, such as sand, borax, or silica gel. If you choose to use sand, first wash it in buckets until it is perfectly clean. Then drain the water and dry the sand thoroughly. Whatever the drying medium you select, the procedure is essentially the same. First, spread a thin layer of medium over the bottom of a wide, shallow container. Place the flowers in the powder so that the blossoms don't touch. Gently pour the drying medium over and around the flowers until they are completely buried. Leave the containers to stand in a warm, dry room. The materials will be dry in three days to one week. Lift the dried flowers very carefully from the medium, and use a soft brush to clean away remaining granules.

Certain plants do not dry well and need to be treated with a preservative. Infusing a glycerine solution into leaves and berries preserves their natural color and texture. To prepare the plants, remove all damaged leaves or those that have blemishes, then scrape off the bark and split the ends of the wood stems about two to three inches. To infuse them with glycerine follow these steps:

1. Combine one part glycerine with two parts very hot water. Mix thoroughly.

2. Pour mixture into an earthenware or stoneware container.

3. Stand the stems in the glycerine solution. The liquid should be two inches up the stem of the plant.

4. When all of the liquid has been absorbed (This takes a few days) pour in more hot solution until it reaches the original level.

5. When beads of moisture appear on the plant material, infusion is complete. Preservation time varies from less than a week to one month for thick leaved material.

6. Store preserved materials in a cool, dry room.

To preserve berries, immerse them in the glycerine and water solution for two to three weeks.

Top right. Hanging bunches of
artemisium are used to add
lightness and gaiety to wreaths.

Bottom right. A Capriland's staff
member works to create a variety
of dazzling wreaths.

Far right. The dried flower garden
at Caprilands in full bloom. These
flowers will be harvested in the
Fall to provide the raw materials
for wreath-making.

Making a Wreath Base

At Caprilands, we make two basic kinds of wreaths, dried wreaths and living wreaths. We make most of our dried wreaths with bases of silver king artemisia. To construct an artemisia base, we use stems of silver king with the curling tops removed. In addition to an ample supply of stems, you will need a wire wreath frame and a spool of lightweight wire to bind the artemisia to the frame.

Begin by bending the stems evenly around the wire frame, securing them together with wire as you go. Do not wire them too tightly. You will need room to insert sprigs of the silver tips into the base. Cover the back of the base with strands of artemisia to give it a finished look; the front will be covered as you decorate it with textured and colorful herbs. Don't be afraid to beat the base into shape, for it must be an even circle. Remember, a wreath is only as good as its base.

When you are satisfied with your base, begin to cover it by inserting the feather tips of the artemisia branches. We call this process "tipping." You may use individual sprays or prepared bundles. Turn the curls toward the center, working clockwise until the circle is filled. Shape the outside line carefully as you work in order to maintain a good circle. Control stragglers by wrapping wire lightly around the whole wreath and then covering the wire with more artemisia sprays. Save the laciest pieces for the center. Push them firmly into the framework, being careful to maintain a circle. Nothing makes a wreath look scragglier than tips of branches running in all directions.

Decorating

After the base is completed, you are ready to add decorative material. If you are making a flower wreath, flowers with weak stems should be wired before you add them. To wire a flower, you will need a 12-inch length of lightweight florist's wire. Gently but firmly push the end of the wire into the base of the bloom; hold the base of the bloom in one hand, and gradually twist the wire around the stem of the flower; then

it is ready to insert into the wreath base. Push your wired or stiff stemmed flower firmly into the base.

If you are using spices, they need to be pierced and wired. Use a small bit to drill holes in nutmeg and cinnamon; then wire then together in bunches of three with lightweight florist's wire. Cardamom can be pierced with a sturdy needle or stiff wire.

Seed pods with stiff stems can be pushed into the wreath base without being reinforced with wire. Pine cones, though, are heavy and must be securely attached to the wreath by twisting an eight-inch piece of lightweight wire around the stem end of the cone and into the base. Sometimes very small cones can be wired together in bunches. You can also attach pine cones with a glue gun.

To add little bags of spices or potpourri, twist them closed with the fine wire and attach them under the bow of the wreath. Often we wire them into the wreath base and tie a bow over them. For a finishing touch, we usually place a bow at the bottom of the wreath.

To make a hanger for your wreath, twist a piece of wire to form a small loop in the center. Then work the ends of the wire into the framework of the wreath to secure them.

Living Wreaths

A living wreath is made on a wire frame ready available in craft stores. Look for wreath forms made with four concentric circles of wire and cross-braced with wire so that they have some height or depth. Ten-inch frames or larger work best for living wreaths.

Sphagnum moss grows wild in bogs and brooks, but you can purchase it at a garden center. It comes in five or ten-pound packages. To make a wreath base, pack the frame with moss and then soak the moss thoroughly with water. Then begin inserting the plants.

Living wreaths must be put on trays to hold moisture and to make watering possible. A round aluminum or stainless steel tray is the most practical, and the rim of the tray frames the wreath nicely. If kept moist, a living wreath lasts almost indefinitely. Water the moss at least once a week. If sun hits it, water it every three days. Do not let it dry out.

Far left, top. A living wreath is for garden display.

Far left, bottom. An incense wreath uses spices to keep sweet-smelling for many months.

Left. A wreath of dried oak leaves is a potent image of autumn.

Making Garlands

Garlands can be made from materials collected from flowering fields or from your garden. Start by braiding together wild flowers, such as daisies, with ferns and grasses. Insert clusters of clovers and daisies into each strand; they will create a lovely background for other colorful flowers you may wish to add.

You may also bind a few stems of flowers or grasses together with fine wire. Knot the wire firmly around the stems, take several turns around the length of the stems, and finish with a knot, but do not cut the wire. Position a second bunch of flowers over the stems of the fist and continue, first tying a knot, then wrapping the stems, this time joining the stems of both bunches. Secure with a knot before adding a third bunch. Proceed until the flower rope is of desired length.

Tools and Supplies

Having a nice work space and the right supplies and tools, makes the craft of wreath making easier and more enjoyable. You will need a large work table in a well-lighted, well-ventilated room. Wreath making tends to be messy,so select a location where you can keep your materials ready and not be concerned about the bits and pieces that scatter about you as you work. Gather the following supplies and have them accessible when you are ready to create your wreaths.

Wire Frames, also called crimped wire rings, are circles of wire made for wreath bases. They are readily available and inexpensive, so we suggest purchasing rather than attempting to make these rings. They come in many sizes. When you are choosing your ring size, bear in mind that to the frame dimension, you will add two or three inches of material, so that the finished size of the wreath on a 10-inch frame easily becomes 12-14 inches.

Special Frames for Advent wreaths include holders for candles. They are readily available in different sizes. Another special frame is the planting frame designed for living wreaths which hold sphagnum moss.

Wire of various weights and types is an absolute necessity. You will need green-coated florist's wire for binding evergreens, and silver wire for artemisia and statice.

A Wire Cutter and Stem Cutter, may be combined in a single tool if you can find one that will cut all materials. The one we use at Caprilands was originally an electrician's tool and works efficiently for both purposes. It has a rounded tip so it can be carried in a pocket. It is steel and self sharpening.

A Glue Gun is helpful when you need to place small, unruly bits into a design.

An Electric Drill is necessary if you are using a lot of cinnamon sticks, ginger roots, nutmegs, and the like. These materials must be drilled and wired before you attach them to the wreath.

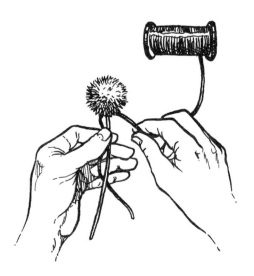

This mantle decoration is a prime example of how wreaths and gar-lands can brighten and bring focus to any room.

46

Appendix A

CATALOG OF HERBS AND FLOWERS

Basil

Ocimum basilicum

Basil is a kitchen herb with a clove-like odor and flavor. Basil grows easily from seed and likes the hottest weather. Harvest frequently from the top to prevent plant from going to seed. Basil for wreaths must be used fresh as it wilts quickly. Insert it with stiff-leafed shrubby herbs such as thyme or sage to hold it in place, or tie in bunches close to the wreath base. Basil signifies honor to the dead, poverty and purification.

Borage

Borago officinalis

Borage is a leafy, many branched herb that produces bright blue, star-shaped flowers. Borage is a hardy annual. Seeds sown either in fall or spring will produce a good stand. Plant borage in full sun. Combine borage with a lemon balm, thyme and salad burnet in a fragrant fresh wreath, or insert the leaves in the moist sphagnum of a living wreath. Borage signifies comfort and courage.

Chamomile

Chamaemelum nobile

Chamomile flowers look like small daisies and the foliage is fine and fern like. Sow seeds in spring in full sun or partial shade, and in well-drained soil. Tie chamomile in compact bunches and force into the

green background of a living wreath. Dried flower heads may be brewed for tea and are appropriate for tea wreaths. Chamomile signifies humility and sweetness.

Caraway

Carum carvi

Caraway is a biennial with finely cut leaves and white flowers that bloom in June of the second year. Sow seeds in September in full sun for an early spring crop. Caraway has many culinary uses and so is appropriate in kitchen wreaths. Seed heads can be used as decoration, and the greens as a wreath base. Caraway signifies protection from theft and brings straying husbands home.

Clover

Trifolium repens and T. pratense

Clover has pink or white globe-shaped flower heads and tender, three leaflet foliage. Clover grows wild and may be harvested throughout the growing season. Soft and pliant chaplets or wreaths may be braided from clover. For a firmer wreath, we add artemisia. Clover was believed to aid in the detection of witches.

Dill

Anethum graveolens

Dill has flavorful, lacy green leaves and decorative seed heads. Sow in early spring and again in July in compost rich soil. Dill may be hung in bunches to dry or thread stems through holes in a box top so seed heads rest on the lid. Use the umbels in witch's wreaths, kitchen wreaths and table decorations. Dill quiets and lulls the spirit.

Elder

Sambucus canadensis

Elder is a stalky shrub that produces clusters of small white flowers and black, shiny berries. Propagate by cuttings or seed in rich, moist soil in partial shade. Elderberries compliment wild wreaths, and the woody branches accent witch's wreaths. Elder was believed to protect against witches.

Artemesium.

Bishop's weed.

Boxwood.

Clover.

Cosmos.

Coxcomb.

Holly.

Johnny jump-up.

Marigold.

Nasturtium.

Nigella pods.

Oak leaf.

Rosehips.

Salvia.

Scented geranium.

Ceedum.

Celusa.

Mugwort daisy.

Geranium.

Michaelmas daisy.

Myrtle.

Rose.

Rose geranium.

Taxus.

Teasil.

Fennel

Foeniculum vulgare

Fennel adds wonderful flavor to foods. The celery-like stems taste like anise. Grow fennel from seed in enriched garden soil. The umbels may be used green or dried. Fennel restores vision, and gives strength in combat.

Geranium, Scented

Pelargonium, spp.

Scented geraniums are only distantly related to the rest of the geraniums. The leaves vary in shape, and their textures range from velvety to sticky. Scents include apple, pineapple, rose and nutmeg. Plant outside as soon as danger of frost has past in dry, well-drained rich soil in full sun. Use scented geraniums in living wreaths or dry away from light between sheets of absorbent paper. Nutmeg geraniums signify an expected meeting.

Goutweed

Aegopodium podagraria

Goutweed is a prolific plant with white and green leaves and a purplish brown stem. A hardy perennial, it spreads rapidly in sun or shade and is often planted as ground cover. The fresh leaves can be twisted into a wreath base, garland, or crown. Decorate with white flowers. Goutweed was believed to ease pain and protect.

Holly

Ilex verticillata

Holly is a shrub with prickly, shiny leaves and bright berries. Holly grows best in the moist air and sandy, slightly acrid soils along the Eastern seaboard. Holly looks best when used fresh in a living wreath. Soaking branches in glycerine will preserve them permanently. Holly was believed to provide protection from witchcraft.

Ivy

Hedera spp.

A wild, vining plant. Some varieties have white and pink coloring in the leaves, others gold. Cuttings from this hardy vine root easily and require very little sun. Use ivy in living wreaths, or twist or braid into a crown. Ivy signifies knowledge.

Lemon Balm

Melissa officinalis

A fragrant green herb with a lemon scent. This hardy perennial may be grown from seed, planted in spring or fall. Lemon balm leaves do not dry well but will last several days in a fresh wreath. Lemon Balm ensures long life and combats melancholy.

Lemon Verbena

Aloysia triphylla

A deciduous shrub with light green, lance-shaped leaves and a delightful, lemony fragrance. Lemon verbena can be trained as a topiary tree. Most plants are grown from cutttings and are not easily propagated. Entire wreaths can be made of verbena. The woody branches can be forced into the base thickly. Decorate with yellow strawflowers. Circle a teapot with a small lemon verbena wreath as it is an important tea ingredient. Lemon Verbena signifies healing.

Lilac

Syringa vulgaris

A woody shrub with green, heart shaped leaves and fragrant white, blue and lavender blossoms. Lilacs need sun and moisture to bloom and must be cultivated from roots in your garden. Use fresh blossoms and leaves in circles around punch bowls in spring. Dried seed heads can be used in autumn arrangements. Lilacs signify love, purity and modesty.

52

A berry-filled, cinnamon wreath welcomes on a wintry morn.

Linden

Tilia americana

Also called basswoods, American lindens can grow to 130 feet. They produce sweet-smelling white to yellow flowers in spring. Lindens can be grown from seed, cuttings, or grafting and do well in most soils but will not tolerate drought. The flowering boughs add fragrance and variety to ordinary wreaths and garlands. The flowering branches were believed to prevent intoxication when worn.

Marjoram

Origanum majorana

A tender perennial with fuzzy, oval gray-green leaves and white or pink flowers in midsummer. Marjoram is grown easily from seed. Little bunches of fresh marjoram can be tied into a kitchen wreath. For Christmas, thread a piece of ribbon through an apple and inserts stems of rosemary, marjoram and oregano into the apple and dangle from a wreath of marjoram. Signifies happiness.

Myrtle

Myrtus communis

A tender shrub with small, decorative leaves and tiny, fragrant white blossoms. Myrtle can be grown outside in the south, but must be grown in pots in the north so it can be brought indoors for the winter. Myrtle has always been used in brides' crowns. Fresh myrtle springs can be twined easily around a wire base and woven together to form a soft crown. Decorate the crown with white roses and white ribbons. Myrtle is the plant of love and virginity.

Parsley

Petroselinum crispum

A small, bright green garden herb with feathery leaves which freshen the breath. Sow seeds in the garden in spring or set out plants. Fresh parsley can be tied easily in bunches and added to a kitchen wreath. Parsley signifies honor and festivity.

Privet
Ligustrum vulgare

An evergreen shrub of the olive family which produces small white flowers and blue-black berries. Privets grow in average soil and can be propagated by cuttings, division, seeds or grafting. Fresh privet branches can easily be twisted into an attractive wreath and are a good substitute for boxwood. Take branches while the flowers are young. Privet signifies love.

Rosemary
Rosmarinus officinalis

A tender perennial evergreen shrub with shining, needle-like leaves. The ginger-like smell so often associated with Christmas is released when the sun hits the leaves or when they are brushed in passing. Rosemary is best started from cuttings and will grow year round unless temperatures drop below 10 degrees F. Small bunches of rosemary are inserted in herb and spice, wedding and Victorian wreaths. Rosemary signifies constancy, fidelity and remembrance.

Rowan
Sorbus aucuparia

Also called mountain ash, the rowan grows to about 30 feet at maturity. Its white spring flowers become decorative clusters of red-orange berries in the fall. Rowan trees can be propagated by seeds or by layering and thrive in most soils. Soak sprays of leaves and berries in glycerine and then use to decorate fall wreaths. The Rowan signifies protection and good luck.

This Christmas decoration of fruits and garlands makes a commanding centerpiece for any room.

Rue
Ruta graveolens

A hardy perennial with bluish green, aromatic foliage and greenish yellow flowers. Its red-brown seed pods look hand carved. Rue is easily propagated from seeds started indoors in the spring. It needs sunlight and a well-drained soil. Rue's seed heads are of decorative value in wreaths, and their strong stems can be inserted in wreaths for an interesting touch. Rue signifies mourning, sorrow and virtue.

Salad Burnet
Poterium sanguisorba

A hardy, evergreen perennial with delicate, attractive leaves similar to the wild rose and which smell like cucumber. The flowers are a deep, but pale crimson. Salad burnet grows easily from seed and thrives in full sun or partial shade. Burnet may be used fresh or dried. Hang stems to dry. Tied in little bunches and attached to wreaths, salad burnet gives off a nice scent. Burnet signifies healing and encourage joy and gladness.

Thyme
Thymus vulgaris

Many varieties of thyme exist today, some creep, some grow upward, some are gray and some are yellow. All have tiny oval leaves, many branches and grow close to the ground. Thyme is a perennial and may be grown from seed in one season. The stems of thyme are too fine and short to force into wreaths, so you should wire cuttings together in small bunches. Small bunches of thyme wired to a frame and tied with a bow make attractive gifts. Add measuring spoons or other small kitchen utensils to the bows as accents. Thyme signifies courage, elegance and energy.

Vervain

Verbena officinalis

Vervain, with its blue flowery spikes, grows along highways in swampy areas. It is quite scarce today. The leaves have a lance-like shape and are deeply divided. Vervain is hard to transplant and difficult to spread or winter over. Try to collect seed from the wild and plant in a moist area. Vervain adds interest to wreaths because of its historical powers of enchantment.

Violets

Viola odorata

Violets have small but exquisite white to lavender and even yellow blossoms and green, heart shaped leaves. Violets are prolific and transplant well. They will self sow. Violets can be dried in silica gel or borax but the best use of violets is in fresh, small dainty wreaths. The stems are strong and pliable, and can be easily twined or braided into a circle. Violets signify modesty, simplicity and honor.

Yew

Taxus spp.

Low-growing yews have broad leaves which are rich and dark green throughout the year, and in the fall produce scarlet berries. Plant in spring before the new growth begins. Yews can be grown in a thin soil but do best in good, enriched earth. Of all evergreens used in holiday wreaths and garlands, yew lasts the longest. The needles do not fall off, and the branches remain oily and pliable. Yew signifies everlasting life.

Right. Autumn at Caprilands is filled with the sights of the harvest.

Below. A pomander tree is the perfect centerpiece for the Christmas table.

Appendix B

CATALOG OF WILD PLANTS

Amaranth, a thick, tall and heart plant which dries well and can be cut to size and shapes into patterns.

Ash, produces interesting keys, or seed-pods

Barberry, displays bright red berries and foliage in fall.

Bayberry, gray-white in color, its cuttings add interest to a greyish wild wreath.

Boneset, the yellowish white blossoms of this herb make excellent additions to floral arrangement.

Dock, can be harvested from the green stage on through its darkest and driest period. When adding dock to wreaths, break the flowering stalk into segments for easy insertion.

Goldenrod, must be harvested early, as soon as the flowers turn yellow. Add them fresh to wreaths or let them dry in the design. Pick before the gold is fully developed.

Hazelnut, works nicely into autumn wreaths designs with pine cones or grasses. The leaves are colorful in fall, and the yellow male catkins are attractive in spring.

Knotweed, the small pink or white blossoms add color when inserted in living wreaths. They also dry well.

Milkweed, produces pods that add a lot of interest to wreaths. We prefer to use them in their natural colors, but they can be gilded or painted for certain projects.

Mullein, the leaves, pressed and dried, and the blossoms, broken in sprigs may be used in wreaths.

Peppergrass, works well in most designs. When dried, it gives a wreath a light, feathery touch.

Queen Anne's Lace, is a handsome weed, with flat, white flower heads resembling lace. Use in delicate wreaths.

Smooth Sumac, adds a distinct red color that is hard to find elsewhere. Break the fruit into small bits and place a wire around the part to be inserted in the wreath.

Spicebush, The bark has a fragrant and spicy odor and produces lovely yellow blossoms in early spring.

Spirea, produces pink flowers that dry very well for use in wreaths.

Sweet Everlasting, harvest mature plants from August to November. Shake the fluff from the plant to uncover a daisy like flower.

Teasel, produces small, purple flowers which are replaced by seed heads that dry brown. These seed heads make find accents in all kinds of herb decorations and wreaths.

Wild Clematis, gather is when the white of the beard begins to show. It dries well and will not lose its fluff.

Witch Hazel, the hard shelled pods shoot out their seeds like bullets from a gun. To harvest, cut the blowers with long stems. They dry well in interesting forms for winter bouquets and the seedpods make nice accents in wreaths.

Yarrow, dries well in bunches and can also be used fresh.